Paleo For Beginners

Paleo Diet – The Complete Guide to Paleo – Paleo Recipes, Paleo Weight Loss

SUSAN PERRY

Table of Contents

Introduction

I want to thank you and congratulate you for grabbing this book *Paleo For Beginners: Paleo Diet – The Complete Guide to Paleo – Paleo Recipes, Paleo Weight Loss.* Making the decision to change your lifestyle for the better is a major step and one for which you should be applauded. Good intentions can't actually make any of the changes suggested within, however, that will take commitment, will power and a true desire for change.

Luckily it won't be all bad, this book contains proven strategies for success along with plenty of delicious breakfast, lunch, dinner and snack recipes to ensure that sticking to the paleo diet is as easy as possible. Remember, it is important to think about committing to a healthy lifestyle as a marathon, not a sprint, slow and steady wins the race. Finally, before you make any major dietary changes you should always consult a nutritionist or health care professional beforehand to ensure you aren't accidentally doing more harm than good.

Thanks again for reading this book, I hope you enjoy it!

CHAPTER 1

The Paleo Diet Explained

Despite what many diets, and even the food pyramid, put forth; the human body just can't handle the amount of carbs that most people consume on a regular basis. It's true, while a lot has changed since the species was little more than hunter-gatherers, the basics of the human body haven't. This means your body is still expecting the type of natural foods it needs to function at its peak, not the processed junk most people fill their bodies with despite knowing it is full of chemicals rather than healthy nutrients.

Switching to a paleo diet means consuming plenty of lean and healthy animal protein from grass-fed and all-natural sources in additional to fowl, fish and lots of dark, leafy greens. One of the best parts of the paleo diet is that you don't have to worry about counting calories or turning your food into points, all you have to do is eat foods that fall within acceptable paleo guidelines and the rest takes care of itself. What's more, during the first few weeks you are transitioning to the paleo diet you will likely see an increase in muscle mass and a decrease of body fat as your body finally starts working at its full potential.

Another benefit of switching to a paleo lifestyle is a natural decrease in the amount of gluten you consume on a regular basis. A recent spotlight on gluten has led to more and more people realizing that they have a gluten allergy which is known to cause a wide variety of issues including those related to digestion, reproduction and even joint pain. Grains themselves are literally trying to send out a message that they should be consumed in moderation; they contain lectin, which is a toxin that is secreted to discourage mass consumption.

As with gluten, dairy is another product that most people just can't handle to the degree that society as a whole might suggest. This is in fact by design, as the enzymes required to digest dairy products properly stop being produced in many peoples' systems as they age out of puberty. Unlike the other paleo guidelines, dairy is one that you have a bit of freedom on. If you are sure it doesn't have any negative effects, then, by all means, consume it in moderation; however, cutting it out for a few weeks, just to see how you feel is always recommended.

Giving up grains doesn't mean giving up carbohydrates, however, it just means that the carbohydrates that you do eat will be of a healthier variety and typically come from vegetables that are naturally high in fiber. It does mean giving up any reliance on refined sugars as, along with many processed foods, it is known to increase the risk of stroke, heart disease and even cancer.

Unfortunately, giving up processed foods with their high amount of unhealthy fats and sugars, can be just as difficult as quitting smoking as your body has long become accustomed to the steady flow of these pleasure inducing substances. This means you will likely experience a decrease in your general energy levels and may even experience symptoms commonly associated with the flu. This is nothing to worry about, however, and it just your body adjusting to your new and improved lifestyle. Stick with it and you will soon feel healthier than you have in years.

The actual amount of carbohydrates your body needs to function properly is around 20 net grams per day. Net grams of carbohydrates are those you take in each day after you subtract out your fiber consumption, but as long as you are eating paleo, you don't even need to worry about the specifics. For comparison, a standard pasta meal at most restaurants contains about 4 times that amount. What this means is that after your body has burned through its extremely high amount of stored carbohydrates, it will have no choice but to start burning fat for part of its fuel source, which is when the real weight loss is likely to begin.

By contrast, a serving of broccoli only has 2 net carbs, which means it is practically impossible to eat an unhealthy amount of broccoli unless you gorge yourself long past any reasonable point of want or need. By simply focusing on all of the foods you can eat, you will quickly lose sight of those unhealthy options your body is not really ready for.

Foods to eat
The following is a list of the foods you will likely want to stock up on before you make the decision to truly try a paleo diet. If the idea of giving up a few of your favorite items is simply too much to bear, consider making a deal with yourself instead. Simply promise yourself that you will go 1 week without the items in question and then reevaluate your position. Odds are, you won't want to go back. All you need to worry about is lean, healthy proteins, healthy fats in moderation, dark, leafy green vegetables and fruits in moderation, there is very little else to it.

Tubers: While the more traditional types of potatoes should be avoided for their high amounts of starches and carbohydrates and relatively low nutritional value, both yams and sweet potatoes are two items you will likely be seeing a lot of moving forward. This doesn't mean they should be consumed recklessly, however, they are still best enjoyed in moderation.

Nuts: Nuts are chocked full of natural energy which makes them a great snack pre or post workout. This energy is generated by their high amount of healthy fats which means you shouldn't consume them to excess. If you find that you aren't seeing much weight loss once you have fully transitioned to the paleo diet, your nut consumption might be to blame.

Fruits: Naturally high in sugar, fruit, regardless of the type, should be consumed in moderation. If you find that you aren't seeing much weight loss once you have fully transitioned to the paleo diet, your fruit consumption might be to blame. The influx of natural sugar can cause your metabolism to go a little haywire, which has been known to make regular, reliable weight loss more difficult.

Oils: Ditch the traditional cooking oil, all organic and all-natural avocado oil and coconut oil are the best choices as are ghee and grass-fed butter if an organic oil is not readily available.

Vegetables: Organic vegetable consumption of any type is strongly encouraged, with the emphasis on dark green and leafy vegetables even more so. Aside from frying them in unhealthy oils, there is little you can do to eat too many of them and they should make up a majority of your diet.

Eggs: High in both omega-3 and protein, organic eggs are a healthy part of the paleo diet as long as they are not consumed to excess.

Chicken/Turkey: Fowl has always been a part of the omnivore's diet, which means that as long as it is organic, and ideally cage free, any type of fowl is great in moderation.

Grass fed animals: As long as the meat is certified as being organic, any grass-fed animal is perfectly acceptable within reason. However, it is vitally important that you go the extra mile and ensure that the animals you are eating were not grain-fed. Grain-fed animals have many of the same problems that people do when it comes to grain, problems that their meat will pass on to you if you give it a chance.

Fish: Studies show that fish, which are farm-raised, are naturally less nutritious and healthy than those that are not. This is particularly noticeable in their decreased Vitamin D levels, as such, it is important to always look for organic, wild fish and consider it a great source of lean protein when not consumed to excess.

Foods to avoid
This a list of all of the foods you will want to remove from your kitchen ASAP and also avoid whenever possible in the future. While going off book and ordering a pizza every now and then isn't going to make the way you generally eat any less healthy, avoiding the following foods will help you feel healthier in the long term.

Processed meat: While many types of meat are a great source of lean protein, processed meats do not fall into that category. The amount of chemicals that the "food" has been subjected to counteracts any health benefits it might once have had and have even been shown to cause asthma in lab mice. The lower quality of the meat as a rule also means it contains fewer nutrients by default and the way it is treated also means it is much higher in sodium and nitrates which are known to cause heart disease and make it difficult for the red blood cells to produce oxygen respectively.

Non-organic tubers: Yams and sweet potatoes that are not certified organic should be avoided whenever possible as they are routinely treated with numerous fungicides and pesticides while in the ground, and even more of the same once they are picked to ensure they stay fresh long enough to make it to your refrigerator. These chemicals are known to increase the risk of Alzheimer's disease, Parkinson's disease, cancer, birth defects, learning deficiencies, asthma and autism.

Nonorganic milk: While milk might be perfectly fine on your digestive tract, milk that is not organic is traditionally treated with numerous types of hormones designed to ensure that each cow is productive as possible. This attitude is also responsible for the acceptable amount of puss that is found in every gallon sold as well. What' s worse is the number of antibiotics those gallons also include which are known to make it more difficult for the body to battle infection. These additions are also known to increase the risk of prostate, breast and colon cancer.

Microwave popcorn: While never considered a health food, even the relatively healthiest type of microwaveable popcorn may be hiding an unfortunate secret, and make no mistake, hiding is definitely the right word. A chemical component of many common butter flavorings is known as diactyl which is also known to lead to lung cancer via the way of bronchitis is inhaled regularly. The worst part is that this chemical falls under the umbrella of ingredients consider artificial flavorings so there is no way to know which brands contain it.

Margarine: Once you decide to make the change to the paleo diet, one of the first things to go from your kitchen should be margarine or any other non-healthy butter or oil substitute. Healthy fats are good for your body and a great source of energy, let them work for you and you won't regret it.

White flour: As a practitioner of the paleo lifestyle, your days of using white flour are over, which is great for multiple reasons; the most important of which, the fact that it is essentially devoid of all nutritional value. The whitening process removes what little it might once have held, and as an added reason it should be avoided, is known to increase the chance of breast cancer in women by over 100 percent.

Eating cheap while eating healthy

Most health food stores have developed a reputation of catering to those with only the most expensive of tastes. While this is true in some cases, when it comes to the majority of the items you will likely eat while following the paleo diet you will find that, with a little initial effort, your grocery bills will remain more or less the same. Don't let the perception of a price barrier hold you back from eating healthy, consider the following suggestions to keep your food budget under control.

Prioritize cheap, healthy eating: While the organic and healthy alternatives at your nearest grocery store are likely not going to be the cheapest around, if you take a bit of extra time to research where the best options in town are, you will likely find a few places with great prices on the items you are looking for. A perfect place to start is your local farmers market, and someone there will likely be able to point you in the right direction for the items you are having more difficultly acquiring.

Plan ahead: Following a paleo diet means that most of the time you are likely going to be making meals yourself to avoid from having to pay for high priced single serving paleo options. This means that you will need to plan out what meals you are going to make in advance as leaving it up to chance can easily leave you in a situation where eating outside the paleo guidelines is the only realistic option. This may take the form of making larger helpings of food for use later or a diet that is more focused on individual natural foods instead of meals. Whatever you decide, planning out your meals will save you time and money in the long run.

Start with the basics: While single serving and imported paleo foodstuffs can quickly scale towards unreasonable on price, the building blocks of any good diet, lean cuts of meat, fruits and vegetables all remain relatively inexpensive, with a little effort and when purchased in large amounts. A kitchen full of the basics will then allow you to splurge on a few items here and there, and really stretch them for maximum effectiveness.

Getting into the habit

After you have made it past the point where your body is craving the types of unhealthy processed foods you once ate, you will begin to find that by following the paleo diet you will have more energy and look and feel healthier than you have in years. This is thanks to the fact that you are finally providing your body with the nutrients it needs to operate as efficiently as possible. Additionally, the complex carbohydrates, lean proteins and healthy fats you are now consuming all come together to make you feel fuller for a longer period of time, making you naturally want to consume additional calories less often without even thinking about it.

Sticking with the paleo diet is guaranteed to offer everyone some type of promising result, but those results will only be long lasting if you commit to following the paleo diet strictly in the long term. This means that if you are still holding out a longing for some processed food or another, you are unlikely to find a direct analog here. If not having access to one or more unhealthy options truly seems to you like it will be too much to handle they the paleo diet might not be for you. The paleo diet offers no "cheat days, or tips and tricks to make the process of transition easier, just the facts regarding the benefits of doing so and the assumption that you have the willpower to stick with it for the long term.

It is important to have an honest conversation with yourself regarding your long term potential for success now, before your body has adapted to the changes you have made too thoroughly. Sticking with the paleo diet for a time, dropping off and coming back around on it will only subject your body to a revolving door of withdrawal symptoms that will make it difficult to get anything done. Do yourself a favor now and determine just how committed you are to finding the healthiest, most energetic you possible.

Every good paleo meal should be comprised of a healthy protein, then paired with a vegetable and a smaller portion of fruit and healthy oils should be used as needed. When you are sticking with the paleo diet, additional restrictions aren't needed. If you find that you are hungry between meals, a healthy snack of a piece of fruit or a handful of nuts is a great choice, if, on the other hand, you feel full when lunchtime rolls around, there is no reason not to skip it. Listen to your body and eat when you feel the need. Once your body has gotten used to your new diet, you are likely to notice a loss of between 1 and 2 pounds each week. If you don't see yourself losing that weight regularly, consider your dairy, fruit and nuts consumption and cut back on areas of excess.

CHAPTER 2

History of the Paleo Diet

Before we delve into the many delicious recipes that can be consumed on the Paleo Diet, it is important that you have a good understanding of the history of Paleolithic nutrition. While you likely understand that the foods included in the Paleo diet have come from a more traditional, caveman-type diet, the ideas that led to the development of the Paleolithic diet are a little more complex. You will be surprised to learn about the rich history of the Paleo Diet. While the idea has been around for decades, you will see that it has taken quite a bit of evolution and a large amount of understanding from the scientific community to reach the conclusions that have been found based on the effects and health benefits that are understood today.

Charles Darwin and Evolutionism

The Paleo Diet evolves heavily based on the diets of our ancestors. Thus, some of the ideas that led to the development of this diet include evolutionism. The ideas of evolutionism and the way that different species developed over time can be tied to the ideas produced by Charles Darwin in his 1859 book, *Origins of the Species*. In this book, Darwin discusses the ideas that would go on to make up the foundation of the topic of evolutionary biology.

Why Evolutionism is Relevant

Evolutionary biology plays a role in the Paleolithic Diet because our own species has evolved over time. As our species evolved and learned new ways of growing, storing, and cooking food, so did the things that humans eat. Dairy, grains, and salts were added to foods and eventually processed foods were manufactured.

While it would make sense that evolved beings would eat the evolved foods, the Paleo Diet is based heavily on eating the foods consumed by our ancestors. Even as you map the evolutionary changes of the human species, various studies and genetic mapping has shown that 99.99% of our genetic make-up still comes from the cavemen that existed in the earlier days of our species.

While man has evolved in many ways since the time of our ancestors, it holds true that our digestive systems have not kept up. As you will see in the following chapter, many of the diseases found in the world today (including heart disease, high blood pressure, and high cholesterol, among others) are a result of the Westernization of people. Many of the diseases that exist today were almost non-existent in the times of our ancestors. It seems, therefore, that even though our bodies and minds have evolved quite a bit from the days of the caveman, it would be better for our total health to stick to the diet that our caveman ancestors followed and avoid the refined grains, processed foods, and dairy products that cause so many health problems and sensitivities among Western populations today.

Weston Price and the Negative Effects of Modern Diets

One of the first books to be published and gain recognition that addressed the modern, Western diet was *Nutrition and Physical Degeneration, A Comparison of Primitive and Modern Diets and Their Effects* by Weston Price. This was published for the first time in 1939 and was a collection of Dr. Price's work. During the 1920s and 30s, Price travelled around the world and observed the diet and health of different populations throughout the world. His work was highly focused on non-westernized groups such as the Polynesians, Alaskan Eskimos, African tribal groups, Canadian Indians, and Australian Aborigines.

The common link between the groups the Dr. Price studied was their lack of processed foods. His research concluded that these non-westernized groups had a diet where vitamins were more easily absorbed. The increased nutrition and lack of processed foods seemed to result in better health statistics throughout the population. His work concluded that the adoption of modern diets by non-westernized cultures led to a decline in overall health.

While Dr. Price's work was interesting, it was unfortunately developed in a time when his ideas were quite advanced. It would still be decades before the Paleo diet that we know today would even be considered as a viable means of achieving optimal health.

Joseph Knowles and His Excursions into the Wilderness

In the year 1930, a man named Joe Knowles went off on his own into the wilderness for 8 weeks, with nothing but a cloth jockstrap to cover himself. He had set out to answer a question: Could modern man survive in the wilderness after nature had made him soft? Knowles wanted to know whether or not he could manufacture weapons and clothing with his bare hands and hunt and kill his own food sources. He wanted to know if men could once again claim his primitive instincts and live in the wilderness.

Knowles would return after 8 weeks with bear skin clothing and plenty of stories. He would go on to publish a memoir and play in a nature drama: both were titled *Alone in the Wilderness*. Knowles would also work as a woodcrafter, an art he learned while in the wilderness. Finally, he would leave behind a mark on those who were interested in evolution and the human diet.

The reason that Joseph Knowles would leave his mark is because he was in great shape and health upon his emergence back into the modern world. Even scientists of the time were interested in how his outing would affect his overall health, particularly the absence of salt from his diet. Upon the conclusion of his two-month excursion, he came back with proof that he was stronger, healthier, and fitter as a result of living in the woods. From here, it was suggested that the modernization that most of the country was undergoing deviated from the human being's natural living environment and was actually less healthy than the ways of living during the time of our ancestors.

Arnold DeVries and Nutrition

DeVries published *Primitive Man and His Food* in 1952. This book focused heavily on ancestral diets and the implications for both mental and physical health. While the term "Paleo" diet had not yet been established, it was one of the first books to place emphasis on how a modern diet can have negative implications for mental health. While it was not incredibly impactful on the field, it was one of the building blocks that would eventually lead to the Paleolithic Diet.

Walter L. Voegtin and the Paleo Diet

The term "paleodiet" was coined by Voegtin in *The Stone Age Diet*, a book that he published in 1975. This book discussed the carnivorous nature of humans and how following a primitive diet would keep us strong. Since the genetic blue print of a human being is so close to that of our carnivorous ancestors, Voegtin believed that eating a diet rich in natural protein sources and easy-to-absorb nutrients from nuts, fruit, and vegetables would be incredibly beneficial to overall health.

Unfortunately, Dr. Voegtin's diet idea did not quite take off. It would take a number of other publications by scientists and health experts in the 1980s and 1990s to bring attention to the diet and it would be the 21st century before the Paleo Diet would become a popular means of achieving optimal health. Some of the most notable books and papers include *Stone Age Diet* by Leon Chaitow, published in 1987 and *The Paleolithic Prescription* by Boyd Eaton, published in 1988.

Perhaps the most influential document of this time would be a paper published by the *New England Journal of Medicine* in 1985. Written by Melvin Konner and Boyd Eaton, *Paleolithic Nutrition* would discuss the principles of diet and lifestyle choices and how they were underlying factors in disease.

Darwinian Medicine

Boyd and Konner's paper would catch the eye and the interest of Drs. Randy Neese and George Williams, both of whom were studying at Stony Brook. They wrote a paper called *The Dawn of Darwinian Medicine*, which was published in the *Quarterly Review of Biology* in 1991. This paper would earn the title of the first scientific publication that addressed the relationship between the evolutionary experiences of our ancestors and the way that modern disease is treated today. It also explored the correlation between modern environments and disease and offered new causes for some medical disorders. *The Dawn of Darwinian Medicine* deeply discussed how modern doctors treat medical problems, particularly the habit of prescribing medication for symptoms rather than treating the disease itself. Neese and Williams stated that treating the symptoms and relieving stress prevents the body's natural efforts to kill the sickness.

For example, consider the way that a fever runs through the body. The body responds to infection with a fever because the higher temperature is intended to wipe out the pathogen. When you use medications to block the fever, you stop your body's natural efforts to combat the disease. While you do make it more comfortable to be sick, you prolong the sickness.

The conclusion of the paper was that there is a strong relationship between the diseases that exist today, our modern diets, and the techniques used in modern medicine. It would leave the impact that our hunter-gatherer ancestry should not be ignored and we must blend this with today's advanced technology for improved overall health.

This paper is still the subject of studies decades later and scientists have just now begun to understand and support the theories found here. Thus, this paper would be another large part of research of the people exploring the Paleo Diet today.

Today, the Paleolithic Diet is the focus of many fitness blogs, programs, and more. It has gained traction in the world of fitness and nutrition and its effects are reflected in the people that follow this diet.

CHAPTER 3

Scientific Studies on the Paleo Diet

While the ideas that would lead to the development of the Paleo Diet manifested themselves almost a century ago, it would be a long time before the modern world was ready for these ideas. For this reason, the majority of the studies concerning the Paleolithic diet and lifestyle were conducted in the past decade or two. Of these studies, all of them pointed to the fact that returning to a prehistoric diet consumed by our ancestors could have positive implications for health. This chapter will review the leading scientific studies on the Paleo Diet and the conclusions that were reached.

Studies of the Non-Westernized Kitavans by Dr. Staffan Lindeberg at Lund University, Sweden

Dr. Lindeberg spent about 25 years studying Paleolithic diets. His particular area of interest involved the Kitavans, who were a non-Westernized population that lived near Papua New Guinea on remote islands. The Kitavans had very little interaction with the modern world and consumed food from the land or the sea surrounding their island. This means that foods of the Western diet such as vegetable oils, refined sugars, dairy, cereals, and processed foods did not exist in the Kitavans' diet.

Dr. Lindeberg studied the health of the population and found that it was generally better than other areas of the world, particularly someone living in a Westernized area. Of the Kitavan population, there are no overweight individuals. Their children and adolescents did not suffer from acne and type 2 diabetes and high blood pressure do not exist.

Additionally, instances of stroke and heart disease are incredibly rare. It was concluded that a diet free of dairy, grains, and processed foods found in Western diets was incredibly beneficial to health and helped to prevent a number of diseases found in the Westernized world.

Dr. Lindeberg's Case Studies

When he was ready to test his hypothesis, Dr. Lindeberg would perform three separate studies. In the first, a study published in 2007, Dr. Lindeberg selected 29 patients, all of which were suffering from heart disease and type 2 diabetes. He separated them into two groups. One of the groups consumed a Mediterranean diet that was made up of low-fat dairy products, oils and margarines, fruits and vegetables, fish, and whole grains, while the other group ate a Paleo diet that excluded the dairy and grain products. Both of the groups had improved their blood glucose tolerance, which is a risk factor for heart disease. While both groups improved, the group of patients on the Paleo diet had improved more than those on the Mediterranean diet.

In 2009, Lindeberg compared the effects of a diabetes diet for people with type 2 diabetes to a Paleo diet. In the diabetes diet, subjects were required to consume an increased amount of whole grains, low-fat dairy products, and fruits and vegetables. They were also required to reduce the amount of animal foods that were consumed. In the Paleo diet, there was no cereal, dairy products, or potatoes; however, they did consume high amounts of fruits, vegetables, meats, and eggs. Rather than testing the two groups separately and comparing the results, each of the test subjects that had diabetes ate the diabetes diet for three whole months. Measurements and levels were taken and then they were required to eat the Paleo Diet for three months. While the diabetes diet did produce some results, the Paleo Diet was found to benefit them even further. It reduced weight loss and waist size, improved blood pressure, triglycerides, and HDL cholesterol, and regulated blood glucose and hemoglobin A1c, which is a marker for control of blood glucose in the long-term.

In 2010, Dr. Lindeberg repeated his study. This time, however, leptin was measured. Leptin is known for its role in appetite regulation and bodyweight. It was shown that the group consuming the Paleo diet had improved more because of the greater leptin changes. Additionally, the Paleo diet was found to be more satiating and satisfying than the Mediterranean diet.

2008 Paleo Diet Study by Dr. Osterdahl

In this study, 14 healthy individuals were put on a Paleo diet. Health statistics, weight measurements, and other markers were taken before these individuals ate the Paleo diet for a phase lasting three weeks. In all of the individuals participating in the study, weight was lost, waist size shrunk, and health improved. Some of the health figures that were measured include blood pressure and plasminogen activator inhibitor, which may play a role in artery clogging. Levels were improved in both of these cases.

The results of this study were published in 2008, but the scientific community questioned it since there was no control group present in this study. However, as you will see shortly, a number of other studies produced very similar results.

Studies of Australian Aborigines Returning to Their Original Diets by Dr. Kerin O'Dea at University of Melbourne

For this study, Kerin O'Dea chose 10 Australian Aborigines as his subjects. All of these men and women were middle-aged and born in the Australian Outback, where they lived as hunter-gatherers in their earlier days. At one point, they had been forced to settle into a more Westernized lifestyle and began consuming Western goods. All ten of his subjects eventually developed obesity, as well as type 2 diabetes.

For the observation period, Dr. O'Dea requested that each of these subjects returned to their lives as hunter-gatherers. They would be studied for seven weeks. During the course of the study, the group was transported to their homeland, which was still isolated. It was agreed that the subjects would eat only foods that could be hunted, gathered, or foraged so the group ate foods of their pasts, including crayfish, shellfish, birds, crocodiles, turtles, kangaroos, figs, yams, and bush honey. At the end of the seven-week period, each individual person lost an average of 16.5 pounds. Triglycerides in the body dropped by an impressive 72% and blood cholesterol dropped by 12%. Finally, glucose metabolism and insulin production were normalized and the type 2 diabetes that these individuals suffered from disappeared altogether. Dr. O'Dea's experiments would be discussed in two separate papers- one published in 2009 and the other published in 2010.

A Comparison of Paleo Diets and Reduced Calorie Diets by Dr. Frasetto

In a study published in 2009, a man named Dr. Frasetto put nine separate individuals on a Paleo diet. Rather than requiring the subjects to eat a lower calorie, Paleolithic Diet, the subjects ate the diet in the same caloric amounts that they normally would. This was intended to prove that the subjects from previous studies were benefiting from a hunter-gatherer diet and not just the reduction in calories.

Dr. Frasetto's work was successful in proving his hypothesis. All of the participants included in his group saw improvements in triglyceride levels, LDL cholesterol, total cholesterol, blood pressure, insulin production and regulation, and arterial function. This study was particularly interesting because the Paleo diet was only followed for a period of ten days before the above results were seen. Additionally, these results were consistent for each individual in the group of nine that was studied by Dr. Frasetto.

In Conclusion

The science behind the Paleolithic Diet and lifestyle is very clear. There have been a number of successful scientific studies in the past decade.

While it is unfortunate that the science world could not grasp the correlation between a Western diet and poor health for several decades, the diet was put to the test eventually and the results showed time and time again that it worked. You can expect no less from an idea that has been discussed, explored, and finally tested after several decades of research from innovative researchers in the health and nutrition field.

It will be interesting to see how the Paleo Diet takes hold in the future. Though it is now quite popular among health enthusiasts, dieticians, and fitness gurus, there is a high likelihood of increased research in the future. Now that the implications have been shown for the relief and even for curing disease such as type 2 diabetes, heart disease, stroke, and many others, it is only a matter of time before our current technology and this newfound knowledge work together to improve human's quality of life.

CHAPTER 4

Breakfast Recipes

Basil and Zucchini Breakfast Frittata

This recipe needs 15 minutes to prepare, requires 35 minutes to cook and will typically make 4 servings.

What to Use
- Black pepper (as needed)
- Salt (as needed)
- Red pepper (.5 tsp. flakes)
- Basil (10 leaves sliced)
- Eggs (1 dozen whisked)
- Garlic (1 clove minced)
- Yellow onion (.5 minced)
- Italian sausage (1 lb. ground)
- Zucchini (3 shredded, all liquid removed)

What to Do
- Start by making sure your oven is heated to 325 degrees Fahrenheit.
- Place a sauté pan on the stove on top of a burner turned to a medium heat before adding in the clove of garlic, onion, and Italian sausage.
- Break up the meat and cook until it has browned thoroughly.

- Remove the pan from the stove and add in most of the basil while leaving some for garnish. Add the eggs before seasoning as desired and adding in the zucchini. Combine thoroughly.
- Place the pan in the oven and let the frittata bake for 25 minutes. Garnish with remaining basil prior to serving.

Strawberry Paleo Muffins

This recipe needs 15 minutes to prepare, requires 30 minutes to cook and will typically make 10 servings.

What to Use
- Walnuts (.3 cups chopped)
- Rhubarb (.3 cups diced)
- Strawberries (.5 cups diced)
- Almond extract (1 tsp.)
- Maple syrup (2 T)
- Eggs (3 whisked)
- Salt (1 pinch)
- Cardamom (.25 tsp.)
- Baking powder (.5 tsp.)
- Baking soda (.5 tsp.)
- Coconut flour (.3 cups)
- Tapioca flour (.3 cups)
- Almond four (.3 cups)

What to Do
- Start by making sure your oven is heated to 350 degrees Fahrenheit.
- Prepare a muffin tin.
- In a mixing bowl combine the salt, cardamom, baking powder, baking soda, coconut flour, tapioca flour and almond flour and whisk well before adding in the walnuts, rhubarb, strawberries, almond extract, almond milk, maple syrup and the eggs and combining thoroughly.
- Add the result to the oven tin and let them bake for half an hour, you will know they are finished when you can stick a toothpick into the center of a muffin and pull it out without encountering batter.
- Cool for 10 minutes prior to serving.

Poppy Seed Paleo Breakfast Bread

This recipe needs 20 minutes to prepare, requires 60 minutes to cook and will make 1 loaf.

What to Use-Sauce
- Water (2 T)
- Honey (2 T)
- Lemon juice (2 T)
- Strawberries (1 cup)

What to Use-Bread
- Poppy seeds (2 T)
- Strawberries (.5 cups sliced)
- Eggs (3 whisked)
- Almond extract (2 tsp.)
- Honey (.25 cups)
- Ghee (.3 cups melted)
- Salt (1 pinch)
- Baking powder (.5 tsp.)
- Baking soda (.5 tsp.)
- Arrowroot flour (.25 cups)
- Coconut flour (.25 cups)
- Cashews (1.5 cups ground)
- Zucchini (.5 cups shredded, moisture removed)

What to Do
- Start by making sure your oven is heated to 350 degrees Fahrenheit.
- Prepare a bread pan (9x5).
- In a bowl, combine the salt, baking powder, baking soda, arrowroot flour, coconut flour and ground cashews.
- In a separate bowl, combine the eggs, almond extract, honey and ghee.

- Combine the two bowls and mix well before adding in the poppy seeds and zucchini and mix well before smoothing and folding in the strawberries.
- Add the results to the pan and smooth into shape before placing the pan in the oven and letting it cook for 60 minutes. You will know it is finished when you can stick a toothpick into the center and pull it out without encountering batter.
- Let the loaf cool for 10 minutes prior to slicing.
- To make the sauce, add a saucepan to the stove on top of a burner set to a medium heat before adding in the water, honey, lemon juice and strawberries. Once the strawberries have softened, about 10 minutes, add the results to a blender and blend well.
- Strain the sauce and add it to the bread prior to serving.

Paleo Pancakes

This recipe needs 10 minutes to prepare, requires 25 minutes to cook and will typically make 3 servings.

What to Use
- Cloves (.25 tsp.)
- Cardamom (.25 tsp.)
- Allspice (.25 tsp.)
- Ginger (.5 tsp. ground)
- Cinnamon (.5 tsp.)
- Salt (1 pinch)
- Baking soda (.5 tsp.)
- Baking powder (.5 tsp.)
- Arrowroot flour (.5 cups)
- Coconut flour (.5 cups)
- Vanilla extract (1 tsp.)
- Raw honey (2 T)
- Eggs (3 whisked)
- Coffee (.25 cups cold brewed)
- Chai tea (2 bags)
- Unsweetened almond milk (1 cup)

What to Do
- Add the oil to a pan before adding the pan to the stove on top of a burner turned to a medium heat before adding in the chai tea and the almond milk and letting the bag steep for 5 minutes.
- Remove the bags from the pan and the pan from the stove and let it sit for 5 minutes.
- Add the results to a bowl before adding in the spices, salt, baking soda, baking powder, almond flour and coconut flour and combine thoroughly.
- If your dough seems thick, add more almond milk.

- Grease a larger pan and return it to the burner set to a medium heat and let it heat up fully. Ladle on the batter so it will make 9 pancakes total. Each pancake should cook for about 2 minutes on each side
- Top with pecans or maple syrup prior to serving.

Plantain and Chorizo Hash

This recipe needs 15 minutes to prepare, requires 35 minutes to cook and will typically make 4 servings.

What to Use
- Black pepper (as needed)
- Salt (as needed)
- Eggs (8 fried)
- Smoked paprika (.25 tsp.)
- Chili powder (.25 tsp.)
- Oregano (.25 tsp. dried)
- Garlic powder (.25 tsp.)
- Brown plantains (2 peeled, cubed)
- Red bell pepper (1 diced)
- White onion (.5 minced)
- Chorizo (1.5 lbs. ground)
- Bacon (3 pieces chopped)

What to Do
- Place the bacon in a pan before adding the pan to the stove on top of a burner turned to a medium heat.
- Cook the bacon as desired before removing it from the pan and adding in the bell pepper, white onion and chorizo, breaking up and browning the meat at the same time.
- Cook for 10 minutes before removing the results from the pan and add in extra ghee if needed before adding in the plantains and letting them cook for 3 minutes and seasoning with paprika, chili powder, oregano, garlic powder, salt and pepper. Cook the other side of the cubes for 3 minutes as well.
- Combine all ingredients and top with fried eggs prior to serving.

Vanilla Paleo Waffles

This recipe needs 10 minutes to prepare, requires 30 minutes to cook and will typically make 3 servings.

What to Use
- Salt (1 pinch)
- Cinnamon (.25 tsp.)
- Baking soda (1 tsp.)
- Vanilla protein powder (1 cup)
- Arrowroot flour
- Coconut oil (2 T melted)
- Vanilla extract (1 tsp.)
- Eggs (4 whisked)
- Applesauce (.75 cups)

What to Do
- In a mixing bowl, combine the coconut oil, vanilla extract, eggs and applesauce and mix well. Mix in the arrowroot flour, the salt, cinnamon and baking soda and combine thoroughly.
- Pour the resulting batter into your waffle iron and cook as needed, an average of 5 minutes per waffle should suffice.
- Top with maple syrup or coconut whipped cream prior to serving.

Paleo Breakfast Bowl

This recipe needs 5 minutes to prepare, requires 0 minutes to cook and will typically make 3 servings.

What to Use-Base
- Vanilla extract (.5 tsp.)
- Raw honey (1 tsp.)
- Cocoa powder (1 T)
- Sunflower seed butter (2 T)
- Chocolate protein powder (1 scoop)
- Almond milk (2 cups)
- Bananas (3)

What to Use-Toppings
- Bananas (1 chopped)
- Cacao nibs (.25 cups)
- Almonds (.3 cups chopped)
- Paleo granola (.3 cups)
- Coconut flakes (.3 cups)

What to Do
- In a blender, add the vanilla extract, raw honey, cocoa powder, sunflower seed butter, protein powder, almond milk and bananas into a blender and blend well.
- Add the results to 3 bowls and add in the toppings prior to serving.

Chia Coffee Breakfast Bowl

This recipe needs 8 hours to prepare, requires 0 minutes to cook and will typically make 3 servings.

What to Use-Base
- Chia seeds (1 T + .25 cups)
- Maple syrup (1 T)
- Cocoa powder (1 T)
- Chocolate protein powder (2 T)
- Vanilla extract (1 tsp.)
- Almond butter (1 T)
- Almond milk (1 cup)
- Coffee (.5 cups brewed, chilled)

What to Use-Toppings
- Bananas (1 chopped)
- Cacao nibs (.25 cups)
- Almonds (.3 cups chopped)
- Paleo granola (.3 cups)
- Coconut flakes (.3 cups)

What to Do
- In a blender, combine the maple syrup, cocoa powder, protein powder, vanilla extract, almond butter, almond milk and coffee and blend well.
- Add the results to a large jar with a resalable lid before adding in the chia seeds. Ensure the jar is firmly sealed before shaking the jar and letting it sit in the refrigerator overnight.
- Add the flavored chia seeds to a microwavable bowl and heat for 30 seconds before adding in toppings as desired.

Poppy Seed Pancakes

This recipe needs 10 minutes to prepare, requires 20 minutes to cook and will typically make 3 servings.

What to Use
- Coconut oil (2 T)
- Poppy seeds (3 T)
- Salt (1 pinch)
- Baking soda (.5 tsp.)
- Baking powder (.5 tsp.)
- Arrowroot flour (.5 cups)
- Coconut flour (.5 cups)
- Lemon juice (1 lemon)
- Lemon zest (1 lemon)
- Vanilla extract (1 tsp.)
- Raw honey (2 T)
- Unsweetened almond milk (.75 cups)
- Eggs (3 whisked)

What to Do
- In a mixing bowl, combine the lemon juice, lemon zest, vanilla extract, raw honey, almond milk and eggs together before adding the following while still whisking, a pinch of salt, baking soda, baking powder, arrowroot flour and coconut flour.
- Ensure the ingredients are thoroughly combined before folding in the poppy seeds.
- Add the coconut oil to a pan before placing it over a burner set to a medium heat. Add the batter to the hot pan, there should be enough for 9 pancakes. Cook each side of each pancake for about 2 minutes.
- Top with maple syrup prior to serving.

Paleo Breakfast Pizza

This recipe needs 10 minutes to prepare, requires 65 minutes to cook and will typically make 3 servings.

What to Use
- Bell peppers (3 sliced in half, seeded)
- Pizza sauce (.5 cups)
- Salt (as needed)
- Pepper (as needed)
- Eggs (6 whisked)
- Basil (4 leaves torn)
- Mushrooms (1 cup chopped)
- Italian sausage (1 lb. ground)

What to Do
- Start by making sure your oven is heated to 325 degrees Fahrenheit.
- Grease a baking dish (8x8)
- Place the bell pepper halves in the baking dish with the skin facing down.
- Add the oil to the frying pan before adding the pan to the stove on top of a burner turned to a medium heat. Add in the Italian sausage and brown it as normal before adding in the mushrooms and letting them soften.
- Add in the basil as well as the pizza sauce and season as needed.
- Mix in the eggs before adding the results to the bell pepper halves.
- Bake the bell peppers halves for about 45 minutes.
- Let cool for 5 minutes prior to serving.

Streusel Muffins

This recipe needs 10 minutes to prepare, requires 30 minutes to cook and will typically make 9 servings.

What to Use-Muffins
- Lemon juice (1 tsp.)
- Vanilla extract (1 tsp.)
- Eggs (3 whisked)
- Almond milk (.25 cups)
- Pumpkin puree (.25 cups)
- Applesauce (.3 cups)
- Apple (1 diced)
- Salt (1 pinch)
- Apple pie spice (.5 tsp.)
- Baking powder (.5 tsp.)
- Baking soda (.5 tsp.)
- Coconut sugar (.5 cups)
- Tapioca flour (.5 cups)
- Coconut flour (.5 cups)

What to Use-Streusel
- Caramel (2 T melted)
- Ghee (2 T)
- Maple sugar (3 T)
- Almond flour (2 T)
- Tapioca flour (1 T)

What to Do
- Start by making sure your oven is heated to 350 degrees Fahrenheit.
- Prepare a muffin tin.

- Combine the apple, salt, apple pie spice, baking soda, baking powder, tapioca flour and coconut flour together in a large bowl before mixing in the remaining ingredients and combining thoroughly.
- Add the results to the muffin tin.
- In a small bowl, combine the tapioca flour, almond flour, maple sugar, ghee and caramel together and add 1 tsp. to each muffin.
- Bake for half an hour and top with the remaining streusel prior to serving.

Paleo, Pumpkin, Protein Smoothie

This recipe needs 5 minutes to prepare, requires 0 minutes to cook and will typically make 2 servings.

What to Use
- Vanilla protein powder (1 scoop)
- Pumpkin pie spice (.5 tsp.)
- Maple syrup (1 T)
- Almond milk (1 cup)
- Pumpkin puree (.3 cups)
- Banana (1)

What to Do
- Combine all of the ingredients together and blend well.
- Consume immediately for best results.

Breakfast Sausage with Fennel and Apple

This recipe needs 10 minutes to prepare, requires 25 minutes to cook and will typically make 4 servings.

What to Use
- Black pepper (as needed)
- Salt (as needed)
- Coconut oil (3 T)
- Rosemary (.5 tsp. dried)
- Red pepper flakes (.5 tsp.)
- Sage (.5 tsp. ground)
- Sea salt (1 tsp.)
- Paprika (1 tsp.)
- Onion powder (1 tsp.)
- Garlic powder (1 tsp.)
- Maple syrup (2 T)
- Red apple (.5 diced)
- Pork (1 lb. ground)
- Fennel seeds (2 tsp.)

What to Do
- Add a small pan to the stove on top of a burner turned to a medium heat. Add in the fennel seeds and let them toast until they become fragrant, about 5 minutes.
- In a mixing bowl, combine the pepper, salt, rosemary, red pepper flakes, sage, paprika, onion powder, garlic powder, maple syrup, red apple, pork and toasted fennel seeds together and combine thoroughly.
- Form the results into patties
- Place the oil in a skillet and place the skillet on the stove on top of a burner turned to a low heat. Cook each patty for 5 minutes on each side.
- Let cool briefly prior to serving.

Sweet Potato and Chicken Bake

This recipe needs 10 minutes to prepare, requires 70 minutes to cook and will typically make 4 servings.

What to Use
- Black pepper (as needed)
- Salt (as needed)
- Eggs (10 whisked)
- Paleo pesto (3 T)
- Chicken (2 cups cooked, diced)
- Garlic (2 cloves minced)
- Yellow onion (.5 minced)
- Sweet potato (1 diced, peeled)
- Coconut oil (4 T divided)

What to Do
- Start by making sure your oven is heated to 400 degrees Fahrenheit.
- Using half of the coconut oil, coat the sweet potatoes before placing them on a baking sheet covered with parchment paper.
- Place the baking sheet in the oven and let the sweet potatoes cook for 25 minutes before removing them from the oven and turning the temperature to 350 degrees Fahrenheit.
- Add the remaining oil to the frying pan before adding the pan to the stove on top of a burner turned to a medium heat. Add in the garlic and onion and let them cook for 5 minutes or until you can see through the onion.
- Mix in the diced chicken and let it cook for 10 minutes before adding in the pesto and combining thoroughly.

- Prepare a baking dish (8x8) by greasing it before adding the results from the pan to it and adding in the salt, eggs and sweet potatoes and mixing well.
- Add the results to the oven and let them cook for 30 minutes.
- Let cool for 5 minutes prior to serving.

Raspberry Breakfast Smoothie

This recipe needs 5 minutes to prepare, requires 0 minutes to cook and will typically make 3 servings.

What to Use
- Himalayan pink salt (1 pinch)
- Gelatin (1 T)
- Coconut cream (1 T)
- Almond milk (1.5 cups)
- Bananas (1 cup chopped)
- Orange juice (1.5 cups)
- Raspberries (1 cup)

What to Do
- Start by placing the orange juice and raspberries into a blender and mixing well. Set the results aside.
- Place the salt, gelatin, coconut cream, almond milk and bananas together in the blender and blend well.
- Place the results into serving glasses and pour in the raspberry mixture on top before swirling with a straw and serving.

Paleo Banana Bread Bars

This recipe needs 5 minutes to prepare, requires 25 minutes to cook and will typically make 9 servings.

What to Use
- Almond (.25 cups sliced)
- Cacao nibs (.3 cups)
- Salt (.25 tsp.)
- Baking soda (.5 tsp.)
- Arrowroot flour (.25 cups)
- Vanilla protein powder (.3 cups)
- Almond flour (.6 cups)
- Egg (1 whisked)
- Vanilla extract (1 tsp.)
- Coconut sugar (.25 cups)
- Coconut oil (.25 cups melted)
- bananas (2 mashed)

What to Do
- Start by making sure your oven is heated to 350 degrees Fahrenheit.
- Prepare a baking dish (8x8)
- In a mixing bowl, combine the salt, baking soda, arrowroot flour, vanilla protein powder, almond flour, egg, vanilla extract, coconut sugar, coconut oil and bananas.
- Add in the cacao nibs before adding the batter to the baking dish and topping with almonds.
- Place the baking dish in the oven and let it cook for 25 minutes or until its middle is fully set.
- Let it sit for 5 minutes prior to serving.

Banana Bread Espresso Muffins with Chocolate Chips

This recipe needs 5 minutes to prepare, requires 25 minutes to cook and will typically make 12 servings.

What to Use
- Mini chocolate chips (.25 cups)
- Salt (1 pinch)
- Cinnamon (1 tsp.)
- Baking powder (.5 tsp.)
- Baking soda (.5 tsp.)
- Coffee grounds (1 tsp.)
- Coconut flour (.25 cups)
- Almond butter (.5 cups)
- Eggs (3 whisked)
- Vanilla extract (1 tsp.)
- Maple syrup (.3 cups)
- Bananas (3 mashed)

What to Do
- Start by making sure your oven is heated to 350 degrees Fahrenheit.
- Prepare a muffin tin.
- Combine the almond butter, eggs, vanilla extract, maple syrup and bananas together in a mixing bowl and combine well before adding in the chocolate chips, salt, cinnamon, baking powder, baking soda, coffee ground and coconut flour.
- Add the results to the muffin tin and place the muffin tin in the oven for 26 minutes.
- Let the muffins cool before removing them from the tin and topping with powdered sugar.

CHAPTER 5

Lunch Recipes

Chicken Fajita Salad

This recipe needs 3 hours to prepare, requires 20 minutes to cook and will typically make 3 servings.

What to Use-Dressing
- Black pepper (as needed)
- Salt (as needed)
- Raw honey (1 T)
- Red wine vinegar (.25 cups)
- Extra virgin oil (.5 cups)
- Garlic (2 heads roasted)

What to Use-Chicken and Marinade
- Agave tequila (1 oz.)
- Cilantro (.25 cups minced)
- Raw honey (3 T)
- Lime juice (1 lime)
- Lime zest (1 lime)
- Olive oil (3 T)
- Garlic (3 cloves sliced)
- Jalapeno (1 chopped)
- Cumin (.25 tsp.)
- Smoked paprika (.5 tsp.)

- Chili powder (.5 tsp.)
- Garlic powder (1 tsp.)
- Oregano (1 tsp. dried)
- Salt (1 tsp.)
- Chicken breasts (3 butterflied)

What to Use- Salad
- Green onion (1 chopped)
- Romaine lettuce (1 head chopped)
- Avocado (1 sliced)
- Yellow bell pepper (.5 sliced)
- Red bell pepper (1 sliced)
- Red onion (.5 sliced)

What to Use-Salsa
- Salt (1 pinch)
- Raw honey (1 T)
- Lime juice (1 tsp.)
- Jalapeno (.5 minced)
- Tomatillos (1 cup diced)
- Strawberries (1 cup diced)

What to Do
- Start by making sure your oven is heated to 400 degrees Fahrenheit.
- Wrap the heads of garlic in foil with a dash of coconut oil and let them bake for 40 minutes.
- Add the resulting baked cloves along with the other dressing ingredients to a blender and blend well.
- Add the chicken to a sealable dish before adding in all of the marinade ingredients and let the chicken marinade for at least 3 hours.
- Grease your grill and turn it to a high heat. Add the chicken and grill each side for 4 minutes or until it has reached an internal

temperature of 165 degrees Fahrenheit.
- Place a pan on the stove over a burner turned to a high heat before adding in a T of coconut oil and the onion and peppers and cooking for 5 minutes.
- Combine all of the salsa ingredients in a small bowl.
- Combine all of the finished ingredients prior to serving.

Grilled Peach and Shrimp Salad

This recipe needs 15 minutes to prepare, requires 15 minutes to cook and will typically make 4 servings.

What to Use-Pesto
- Black pepper (as needed)
- Salt (as needed)
- Lemon juice (2 tsp.)
- Olive oil (.5 cups)
- Garlic (2 cloves minced)
- Basil (1.5 cups torn)
- Pistachios (1 cup unsalted)

What to Use-Salad
- Pistachios (.3 cups unsalted)
- Cherry tomatoes (1 cup halved)
- Cucumber (1 sliced)
- Mixed greens (5 cups)
- Peaches (3 chopped in half, pits removed)
- Garlic powder (to taste)
- Salt (to taste)
- Shrimp (1 lb. deveined, peeled)
- Ghee (2 T divided, melted)

What to Use-Dressing
- Black pepper (to taste)
- Salt (1 pinch)
- Dijon mustard (1 T)
- Raw honey (1 T)
- Lemon juice (.25 cups)
- Olive oil (.5 cups)

What to Do-Shrimp
- In a food processor, add in the pistachios and pulse well before adding in the cloves of garlic as well as the basil. Process again before adding in the olive oil while pulsing until the pesto reaches the desired thickness before mixing in the lemon juice.
- Add the oil to a pan before adding the pan to the stove on top of a burner turned to a medium heat. Add in half of the ghee before adding in the shrimp and seasoning as desired.
- Let the shrimp cook in the pan for 60 seconds per side before adding in 2 T pesto and coating well.

What to Use-Salad
- Add a pan for grilling to a burner set to a medium heat before greasing the peaches with the remaining ghee and grilling each peach for 1.5 minutes per side.
- Combine all of the salad ingredients together as desired.
- Combine all of the dressing ingredients in a jar and shake well before topping the salad.

Paleo Salad with Maple and Apple Vinaigrette Dressing

This recipe needs 20 minutes to prepare, requires 35 minutes to cook and will typically make 4 servings.

What to Use-Salad
- Black pepper (as needed)
- Salt (as needed)
- Apple (2 diced)
- Pecans (.3 cups chopped)
- Cranberries (.3 cups dried)
- Red onion (.5 diced)
- Chicken (2 cups cooked, diced)
- Arugula (4 cups)
- Romaine hearts (2 heads, chopped, rinsed)
- Bacon (4 strips)
- Eggs (4)
- Garlic powder (1 pinch)
- Salt (1 pinch)
- Ghee (2 T)
- Balsamic vinegar (1 T)
- Butternut squash (1 peeled, diced)

What to Use-Dressing
- Black pepper (to taste)
- Salt (to taste)
- Olive oil (.25 cups)
- Shallot (1 tsp. minced)
- Garlic (1 tsp. minced)
- Dijon mustard (1 tsp.)
- Apple cider vinegar (1 T)
- Maple syrup (2 T)

What to Do

- Start by making sure your oven is heated to 400 degrees Fahrenheit.
- On a baking sheet covered with parchment paper, toss the squash in the balsamic vinegar as well as the ghee before seasoning with garlic powder and salt.
- Place the baking sheet in the oven and let the squash cook for 20 minutes.
- As the squash cooks, fill a medium sized pot with water and place in over a burner set to a high heat. After the water boil, add in the eggs and let them boil 15 minutes. After that, remove them from the hot water and place them in cold water. After they have cooled, peel and then chop them.
- Place the bacon in a pan and place the pan over a medium heat. Let the bacon cook as desired before crumbling it into pieces.
- To make the dressing, combine all of the ingredients in a jar and shake well.
- Combine all ingredients as desired and top with dressing prior to serving.

Berry Salad with Chicken

This recipe needs 10 minutes to prepare, requires 30 minutes to cook and will typically make 4 servings.

What to Use-Dressing
- Black pepper (as needed)
- Salt (as needed)
- Poppy Seeds (1 T)
- Garlic (1 clove minced)
- Honey (1 T)
- Balsamic vinegar (2 T)
- Olive oil (.25 cups)
- Strawberries (1 cup sliced)

What to Use-Salad
- Goat cheese (4 oz.)
- Walnuts (.25 cups chopped rough)
- Red onion (.25 sliced thin)
- Blueberries (.5 cups)
- Strawberries (.5 cups sliced)
- Mixed greens (5 cups)
- Chicken (2 cups cooked, cubed

What to Do
- In a blender, combine the garlic clove, raw honey, balsamic vinegar, olive oil and strawberries and blend for 60 seconds.
- Add the results to a jar before adding in the poppy seeds and shaking well.
- Refrigerate for 60 minutes prior to serving.
- In a salad bowl, combine the chicken, goat cheese, walnuts, red onion, blueberries, strawberries and mixed green and coat with the dressing prior to serving.

Chicken Salad with Coconut Thai Sauce

This recipe needs 10 minutes to prepare, requires 15 minutes to cook and will typically make 2 servings.

What to Use-Dressing
- Black pepper (as needed)
- Salt (as needed)
- Red pepper flakes (.5 tsp.)
- Ginger (1 tsp.)
- Garlic (2 cloves chopped)
- Lime juice (1 T)
- Coconut aminos (1 T)
- Coconut vinegar (1 T)
- Cilantro (2 T chopped)
- Olive oil (2 T)
- Raw honey (2 T)
- Sunflower seed butter (.25 cups)

What to Use-Salad
- Coconut (.25 cups shredded, unsweetened)
- Cucumber (1 diced)
- Mixed greens (6 cups)
- Sweet potato (2 cups shredded)
- Black pepper (.25 tsp.)
- Garlic powder (.25 tsp.)
- Sea salt (.25 tsp.)
- Chicken breast (.5 lbs. boneless, skinless, well-pounded)
- Coconut oil (4 T divided)

What to Do
- Start by making the dressing and adding the red pepper flakes, salt, ginger, garlic, pepper, lime juice, coconut aminos, coconut

vinegar, cilantro, olive oil, raw honey and sunflower seed butter into a food processor and processing well. Let it sit in the refrigerator prior to use.

- Add 2 T coconut oil to a pan before adding the pan to the stove on top of a burner turned to a medium heat. Add in the chicken and season as desired before letting it cook for 3 minutes on each side until it reaches an internal temperature of 165 degrees Fahrenheit.
- Add the remaining coconut oil to a spate small pan before adding in the sweet potato, seasoning as needed and cooking it for 5 minutes.
- Let the chicken sit for 3 minutes prior to slicing.
- Combine all of the ingredients and top with dressing prior to serving.

Paleo Squash Soup

This recipe needs 15 minutes to prepare, requires 40 minutes to cook and will typically make 6 servings.

What to Use
- Black pepper (as needed)
- Salt (as needed)
- Lemon juice (2 tsp.)
- Salt (1 tsp.)
- Rosemary (1 tsp. dried)
- Oregano (1 tsp. dried)
- Thyme (1 tsp. dried)
- Chicken bone broth (32 oz.)
- Yellow squash (2 chopped)
- Zucchini (2 chopped)
- Garlic (3 cloves minced)
- Sweet onion (1 minced)
- Ghee (3 T)
- Parsley (1 handful)

What to Do
- Place a Dutch oven on the stove on top of a burner turned to a medium heat. Add in the squash, zucchini, garlic and onion before letting everything cook for 10 minutes or until you can see through the onion.
- Mix in the salt, pepper, rosemary, oregano, thyme and bone broth and cook everything for 20 minutes until both the squash and zucchini are properly tender.
- Remove the Dutch oven from the stove before letting the contents cool and adding them to a blender. Mix in the parsley as well as the lemon juice and blend well.
- Garnish with olive oil and extra parsley prior to serving.

Shrimp and Cauliflower Chowder

This recipe needs 15 minutes to prepare, requires 40 minutes to cook and will typically make 5 servings.

What to Use
- Black pepper (as needed)
- Salt (as needed)
- Parsley (.25 cups chopped rough)
- Bay leaves (2)
- Chicken broth (6 cups)
- Thyme (1 tsp. dried)
- Oregano (1 tsp. dried)
- Smoked paprika (1 tsp.)
- Garlic powder (1 tsp.)
- Garlic (2 cloves chopped)
- Yellow onion (1 chopped)
- Celery (4 stalks diced)
- Carrots (2 diced, peeled)
- Shrimp (1 lb. deveined, peeled)
- Bacon (1.5 lbs.)
- Cauliflower (1 head florets, steamed, pureed)

What to Do
- Place a Dutch oven on the stove on top of a burner turned to a medium heat. Add in the bacon and let it cook until it reaches the desired level of crispness. Remove the bacon from the oven and add in the shrimp before seasoning as needed and cooking each side for 2 minutes.
- Add in the garlic, onion, celery and carrots and toss them in the bacon fat. After you can begin to see through the onion, mix in the salt, thyme, oregano, smoked paprika and garlic powder and stir for 60 seconds.

- Mix in the bay leaves as well as the chicken broth and the cauliflower. Mix in half of the cooked bacon and let it cook for 15 minutes.
- Take the bay leaves out of the mixture before adding in the parsley and pureeing everything in the Dutch Oven.
- Add in the shrimp and heat completely.
- Garnish with parsley, olive oil and bacon prior to serving.

Sweet Potato Soup with Ham

This recipe needs 15 minutes to prepare, requires 8 hours to cook and will typically make 6 servings.

What to Use
- Black pepper (as needed)
- Salt (as needed)
- Chicken bone broth (64 oz.)
- Ham (2 cups diced, cooked)
- Bay leaves (3)
- Thyme (2 T minced)
- Tarragon (2 T minced)
- Parsley (3 T minced)
- Sweet Potatoes (2 diced, peeled)
- Celery (3 stalks diced)
- Carrots (2 diced, peeled)
- Yellow onion (.5 minced)
- Ham bone (1)
- Coconut milk (3 T)

What to Do
- Place the ham bone at the bottom of a slow cooker before adding in the chicken bone broth, the ham, the bay leaves, thyme, tarragon, parsley, sweet potatoes, celery, carrots and onion. Or, you can roast the vegetables beforehand for extra flavor.
- Cover the slow cooker and let it cook for at least 8 hours on a low heat.
- Remove the bone and the bay leaves, add in 3 T coconut milk and mix well prior to serving.

Pomegranate, Bacon and Cauliflower Soup

This recipe needs 10 minutes to prepare, requires 20 minutes to cook and will typically make 6 servings.

What to Use
- Black pepper (as needed)
- Salt (as needed)
- Truffle oil (1 tsp.)
- Pomegranate seeds (.5 cups)
- Sage (6 leaves)
- Bacon (4 pieces)
- Garlic powder (1 tsp.)
- Thyme (1 sprig)
- Truffle salt (1 tsp.)
- Chicken bone broth (32 oz.)
- Cauliflower (1 head florets)
- Garlic (3 cloves sliced)
- Shallots (2 sliced)
- Ghee (2 T)

What to Do
- Add the oil to a saucepan before adding the pan to the stove on top of a burner turned to a medium heat. Add in the ghee as well as the garlic and the shallots and let them cook for 60 seconds before adding in the thyme, truffle salt, chicken bone broth and cauliflower before letting everything cook for 15 minutes.
- As the cauliflower is cooking, cook the bacon in a separate pan also placed over a burner turned to a medium heat and cook until it achieves desired crispiness. Remove it from the pan and crumble it.

- Add the sage to the bacon pan and let it cook for 25 seconds per side.
- After the cauliflower has cooked completely, blend all of the ingredients in its pan.
- Combine all of the ingredients and season as desired prior to serving.

Ginger Soup with Meatballs

This recipe needs 40 minutes to prepare, requires 15 minutes to cook and will typically make 4 servings.

What to Use-Soup
- Black pepper (as needed)
- Salt (as needed)
- Ginger (1 tsp. minced)
- Red curry paste (1 tsp.)
- Coconut milk (1 T)
- Vegetable broth (1 cup)
- Acorn squash (3 cut in half)

What to Use-Meatballs
- Coconut oil (3 T)
- Red pepper flakes (.25 tsp.)
- White vinegar (.5 tsp.)
- Ginger (.5 tsp. minced)
- Sesame oil (1 tsp.)
- Fish sauce (1 tsp.)
- Coconut aminos (1 T)
- Cilantro (3 T minced)
- Garlic (2 cloves minced)
- Yellow onion (.25 minced)
- Pork (.5 lbs. ground)
- Beef (.5 lbs. ground)

What to Do
- Start by making sure your oven is heated to 400 degrees Fahrenheit.
- Line a baking sheet using parchment paper before placing the squash with the skin facing upwards and placing the baking sheet in the oven to cook for 35 minutes.

- After 20 minutes, add the red pepper flakes, white vinegar, ginger, sesame oil, fish sauce, coconut aminos, cilantro, garlic, yellow onion, pork and beef to a mixing bowl before combing thoroughly and seasoning as desired.
- Form the results into 20 meatballs and add them to a pan placed over a medium heat and cook each batch of meatballs for 2 minutes on each side.
- Remove the meat of the acorn squash before blending it thoroughly, adding in the remaining ingredients (except the meatballs) and blend again.
- Add the meatballs to the soup and garnish using cilantro prior to serving.

Ceviche, Mahi Mahi and Mango Tacos

This recipe needs 20 minutes to prepare, requires 10 minutes to cook and will typically make 3 servings.

What to Use
- Black pepper (as needed)
- Salt (as needed)
- Paleo Tortillas (3)
- Olive oil (1 T)
- Cilantro (3 T minced)
- Lemon juice (2 T)
- Lime juice (.5 cups)
- Lime zest (1 lime)
- Garlic (1 clove minced)
- Avocado (.5 diced)
- Mango (1 diced)
- White onion (.25 minced)
- Jalapeno (1 minced)
- Red bell pepper (1 diced)
- Mahi Mahi filet (2 diced)

What to Do
- Combine all of the ingredients except the tortillas in a mixing bowl and combine thoroughly.
- Cover the bowl and let it cool in the refrigerator for 3 10 minutes.
- Remove excess liquid using a slotted spoon.

Add the results to the paleo tortillas prior to serving.

Paleo Pasta with Shrimp

This recipe needs 10 minutes to prepare, requires 20 minutes to cook and will typically make 4 servings.

What to Use-Soup
- Black pepper (as needed)
- Salt (as needed)
- Capers (3 T)
- Lemon (1 sliced thin)
- Lemon zest (.5 lemons)
- Chicken bone broth (.5 cups)
- Lemon juice (.5 cups)
- Ghee (4 T + 2T)
- Shallot (1 sliced thin)
- Garlic (2 cloves minced)
- Garlic powder (.25 tsp.)
- Shrimp (1 lb. deveined, peeled)
- Zucchini (3 peeled, spiralized)

What to Do
- Remove the excess water from the zucchini noodles by placing them between a pair of paper towels.
- Place 2 T ghee into a pan before adding that pan to a burner set to a medium heat. Season the shrimp and let the pan heat before adding it in and letting it cook for 1.5 minutes per side.
- Remove them from the pan before adding in the shallot as well as the garlic and letting them cook for 3 minutes.
- Add in the remaining ghee as well as the lemon zest, chicken bone broth and lemon juice and letting the pan come to a low boil.
- Add in the capers as well as the lemon slices and turn the burner to low before cooking for 4 minutes.

- Add the rest of the ingredients into the pan and coat well. Cook for 2 more minutes.
- Garnish with parsley prior to serving.

CHAPTER 6

Dinner Recipes

Loaded Paleo Tacos

This recipe needs 15 minutes to prepare, requires 8 hours and 40 minutes to cook and will typically make 3 servings.

What to Use-Salsa
- Black pepper (as needed)
- Salt (as needed)
- Cilantro (.3 cups packed)
- Lime juice (2 limes)
- Garlic (2 cloves)
- Jalapenos (3)
- Tomatillos (10)
- Ghee (2 T)

What to Use-Beef
- Salt (as needed)
- White onion (.5 sliced)
- Beef bone broth (1 cup)
- Beef tongue (1)

What to Use-Tacos
- Cilantro (1 handful chopped rough)
- Pineapple (1 cup cubed)

- Radish (3 sliced tin)
- Avocado (.5 sliced)
- Paleo tortillas (3)

What to Do
- Ensure that your oven has been preheated to 450 degrees Fahrenheit.
- Using tinfoil, line a baking sheet before placing the jalapenos and tomatillos on it before coating each with ghee and salting as needed.
- Bake for 20 minutes before letting them cool and peeling off the skins and discarding. Add the results to a food processor, add in the remainder of the salsa ingredients and process well. Let the salsa chill overnight.
- Cut three holes for the garlic cloves in the beef tongue before placing the results in a slow cooker along with the onion and bone broth. Cover the slow cooker and let the tongue cook for 8 hours on a low heat.
- Once cooked, skin the tongue and shred it before adding it back into the broth to soak.
- Coat a pan with the ghee and place it on the stove above a burner that has been turned to a high/medium heat. Add in the tongue and let it cook for 2 minutes per side until it is crispy.
- Combine all of the ingredients and wrap in a paleo taco prior to serving.

Marinated Flap Steak

This recipe needs 4 hours to prepare, requires 30 minutes to cook and will typically make 4 servings.

What to Use
- Black pepper (as needed)
- Salt (as needed)
- Coconut oil (2 T)
- Mango Salsa (as needed)
- Cumin (.5 tsp.)
- Coriander (.5 tsp.)
- Lime juice (1 T)
- White onion (.25 minced)
- Olive oil (.5 cups)
- Parsley (1 cup packed)
- Cilantro (1 cup packed)
- Flap steak (2 lbs. sliced thin)

What to Do
- In a food processor, combine .5 tsp. salt, cumin, coriander, lime juice, white onion, olive oil, parsley and cilantro and process well.
- Add the steak and half of the contents of a food processor to a resalable plastic bag before placing in the refrigerator to marinate for 4 hours.
- Let the steak sit at room temperature for half an hour before heating your grill to a high heat and cooking the meat for approximately 2 minutes on each side.
- Top with the remaining marinade prior to serving.

Fajita and Poblano Kabobs

This recipe needs 1 hour to prepare, requires 20 minutes to cook and will typically make 3 servings.

What to Use-Marinade
- Black pepper (as needed)
- Salt (as needed)
- Flank steak (1 lb. sliced thin)
- Red pepper flakes (.25 tsp.)
- Sweet paprika (.25 tsp.)
- Oregano (.25 tsp.)
- Garlic powder (.25 tsp.)
- Lime juice (.5 T)
- Coconut aminos (.25 cups)

What to Use-Kabobs
- Red onion (.5 chopped)
- Red bell pepper (1 chopped)
- Yellow bell pepper (1 chopped)

What to Use-Poblano Pesto
- Coconut oil (2 T)
- Lime juice (.5 T)
- Cilantro (.5 cups)
- Poblano pepper (1 roasted)

What to Do
- Place the marinade ingredients as well as the steak into a dish with a lid and ensure the meat is well coated. Let the marinade chill for at least 2 hours.
- Skewer the meat and vegetables as desired before heating a grill pan in the oil and place it on the stove above a burner that

has been turned to a medium heat. Brush each kabob with the marinade before cooking each side for approximately 4 minutes.
- As the kabobs are cooking, add the pesto ingredients to a blender and blend well.
- Add the pesto to the kabobs prior to serving.

Bulgogi

This recipe needs 8 hours to prepare, requires 30 minutes to cook and will typically make 3 servings.

What to Use-Bulgogi
- Black pepper (as needed)
- Salt (as needed)
- Coconut oil (2 T)
- Hanger steak (1.5 lbs. sliced thin)
- Red pepper flakes (.5 tsp.)
- Coconut vinegar (1 T)
- Pear (.5 grated)
- Garlic (2 cloves minced)
- Raw honey (2 T)
- Ginger (3 T minced)
- Coconut aminos (.25 cups)

What to Use-Cucumbers
- Salt (1 pinch)
- Raw honey (.5 tsp.)
- Chili sauce (1 tsp.)
- Coconut vinegar (2 T)
- Cucumber (1 sliced thin)

What to Use-Rice Bowl
- Cauliflower rice (1 batch)
- Eggs (3)
- Sriracha mayo (.5 cups)

What to Do
- Combine all of the Bulgogi ingredients in a dish with a lid before adding in the beef, coating well and letting it chill for a minimum of 4 hours.

- Add the cucumber ingredients to a jar before adding in the cucumber, sealing the jar and shaking well. Let it sit until the Bulgogi is ready.
- Coat a pan with 2 T coconut oil and place it on the stove above a burner that has been turned to a medium heat. Add in the beef and spread it out in a single layer, cooking for approximately 2 minutes per side.
- Add a separate skillet to the stove over a burner set to a low heat before adding in 1 T coconut oil and cooking the eggs until the whites are cooked but the yolks are not yet hard.
- Combine all of the ingredients and garnish with sesame seeds and green onions prior to serving.

Red Beef Curry

This recipe needs 15 minutes to prepare, requires 25 minutes to cook and will typically make 4 servings.

What to Use
- Black pepper (as needed)
- Salt (as needed)
- Coconut oil (2 T)
- Lime leaves (2)
- Lemongrass (1 stalk)
- Mushrooms (1 cup sliced)
- Broccoli (1 head florets)
- Red bell pepper (1 sliced)
- Coconut aminos (1 T)
- Fish sauce 91 tsp.)
- Red curry paste (2 T)
- Coconut milk (28 oz.)
- Ginger (2 tsp. grated)
- Yellow onion (.5 diced)
- Garlic cloves (3 minced)
- Flank steak (1 lb. sliced thin)

What to Do
- Coat a pan with the oil and place it on the stove above a burner that has been turned to a medium heat. Add in the steak, season as desired and let it brown for 3 minutes.
- Remove the meat from the pan before adding in the ginger, yellow onion and garlic and letting them cook for 60 seconds. Add in 14 oz. of coconut milk before adding in the coconut aminos, fish sauce and curry paste and whisking well.
- Mix in the lime leaves, lemongrass, mushrooms, broccoli and season as needed. Cover the pan and let everything cook for 15 minutes.

- Mix the beef into the pan before adding in the remaining coconut milk and cooking for 2 additional minutes.
- Remove the lime leaves and lemon grass prior to serving.

Chicken and Pineapple Kabobs

This recipe needs 20 minutes to prepare, requires 30 minutes to cook and will typically make 3 servings.

What to Use-Sauce
- Black pepper (as needed)
- Salt (as needed)
- Coconut aminos (.25 cups)
- Ginger (.25 tsp.)
- Garlic powder (.5 tsp.)
- Fish sauce (1 tsp.)
- Chili sauce (1 T)
- Raw honey (1 T)
- Cashew butter (2 T)
- Pineapple (3 cups diced)

What to Use-Kabob
- Garlic powder (.5 tsp.)
- Black pepper (to taste)
- Garlic powder (to taste)
- Salt (to taste)
- Ginger (.5 tsp.)
- Pineapple (1 cup cubed)
- Chicken thighs (2 lb. cubed)

What to Do
- In a blender, combine the ginger, garlic powder, fish sauce, chili sauce, raw honey, cashew butter, lime juice, coconut aminos and pineapple together and blend well to form the sauce for the kabobs.
- Add the sauce to a pan before placing the pan on the stove over a burner turned to a medium heat to allow it to reduce for 10 minutes, whisk regularly.

- Arrange the kabobs as desired before coating a grill pan in the oil and placing it on the stove above a burner that has been turned to a medium heat. Add the kabobs to the pan and let them cook for about 10 minutes, brushing with sauce occasionally.
- Top with sauce prior to serving.

Jerk Chicken

This recipe needs 24 hours to prepare, requires 60 minutes to cook and will typically make 3 servings.

What to Use
- Black pepper (as needed)
- Salt (as needed)
- Coconut oil (2 T)
- Allspice (.5 tsp.)
- Ground cloves (.5 tsp.)
- Nutmeg (1 tsp. ground)
- Cinnamon (1 tsp. ground)
- Ginger (1 tsp. ground)
- Thyme (1 T dried)
- Lime juice (1 T)
- Ghee (.5 cups)
- Coconut aminos (3 T)
- Jalapenos (2 chopped)
- Garlic (4 cloves chopped)
- White onion (.25 chopped)
- Chicken breast (1.5 lbs. skinless, boneless)
- Cinnamon (1 tsp.)
- Brown plantains (3 sliced)

What to Do
- In a blender, combine the allspice, cloves, salt, pepper, nutmeg, cinnamon, ginger, thyme, lime juice, coconut oil, coconut aminos, jalapenos, cloves and white onion together and blend well.
- Add the results to a dish with a lid, add in the chicken and coat well. Let the chicken chill in the marinade for 1 day.
- Ensure that your oven has been preheated to 425 degrees Fahrenheit.

- Place the chicken in a skillet along with the marinade and bake the skillet 15 minutes and the chicken is 165 degrees internally.
- Let it sit for 5 minutes prior to slicing.
- Coat a pan with the oil and place it on the stove above a burner that has been turned to a medium heat. Add in the plantains and top with cinnamon and salt as needed before letting each side cook for 2 minutes.
- Serve the chicken and plantains with cauliflower rice and top with green onions and lime prior to serving.

Butter Chicken

This recipe needs 10 minutes to prepare, requires 30 minutes to cook and will typically make 4 servings.

What to Use
- Black pepper (as needed)
- Salt (as needed)
- Coconut oil (2 T)
- Tomato sauce (1 cup)
- Coconut milk (28 oz.)
- Cumin (.5 tsp. ground)
- Cayenne pepper (.5 tsp.)
- Turmeric (1 tsp.)
- Garam masala (2 tsp.)
- Ginger (1 tsp. minced)
- Garlic (3 cloves minced)
- Yellow onion (1 diced)
- Chicken thighs (2 lbs. cubed)

What to Do
- Coat a pan with the oil and place it on the stove above a burner that has been turned to a medium heat. Add in the chicken and season as desired before cooking all sides for a total of 10 minutes.
- Remove the chicken from the pan before adding in the onions and garlic let them sauté, you will be able to tell when they are finished because the onions will be practically see through.
- Add in the cumin, cayenne pepper, turmeric, garam masala and ginger before letting them cook for half a minute. Mix in the tomato sauce and coconut milk before simmering for 5 minutes.

- Add the chicken back in and let it cook until it reaches an internal temperature of 165 degrees Fahrenheit.
- Pair with cauliflower rice and garnish with lime juice and cilantro prior to serving.

Paleo Chicken Wings

This recipe needs 5 minutes to prepare, requires 30 minutes to cook and will typically make 4 servings.

What to Use
- Black pepper (as needed)
- Salt (as needed)
- Rosemary (2 tsp. minced)
- Raw honey (.25 cups)
- Dijon mustard (.3 cups)
- Chicken wings (2 lbs.)
- Red pepper flakes (to taste)

What to Do
- Ensure that your oven has been preheated to 400 degrees Fahrenheit.
- Place your oven rack in the highest position possible.
- Cover a baking sheet with tinfoil and set a wire rack on top of it. Season the wings as desire before placing the baking sheet in the oven until the wings are crispy, this should take roughly 50 minutes.
- Add a saucepan to the stove over a burner set to a medium heat before mixing in the red pepper flakes, rosemary, honey and mustard and let it warm for 2 minutes.
- Coat the wings in the sauce prior to eating. Serve promptly for best taste.

Chicken Salad with Poppy Seeds

This recipe needs 30 minutes to prepare, requires 0 minutes to cook and will typically make 4 servings.

What to Use-Rolls
- Coconut oil (2 T)
- Eggs (2)
- Egg whites (4)
- Salt (1 pinch)
- Baking powder (.5 tsp.)
- Baking soda (.5 tsp.)
- Coconut flour (.25 cups)
- Arrowroot flour (.5 cups)
- Almond meal (1 cup)

What to Use-Chicken Salad
- Black pepper (as needed)
- Salt (as needed)
- Garlic powder (.25 tsp.)
- Walnuts (.25 cups diced)
- White onion (.25 minced)
- Carrot (.25 cups diced)
- Celery (1 stalk diced)
- Chicken (2 cups cooked)
- Paleo mayo (.25 cups)

What to Use-Dressing
- Black pepper (as needed)
- Salt (as needed)
- Poppy Seeds (1 T)
- Garlic (1 clove minced)
- Honey (1 T)

- Balsamic vinegar (2 T)
- Olive oil (.25 cups)
- Strawberries (1 cup sliced)

What to Do
- To make the biscuits ensure that your oven has been preheated to 350 degrees Fahrenheit.
- In a mixing bowl, combine the salt, baking soda, baking powder, coconut flour, arrowroot flour and almond meal.
- Beat the egg whites in a separate bowl before adding them to the mixing bowl followed by the coconut oil and remaining eggs.
- Let the batter cool for half an hour before portioning the dough onto a lined baking sheet. Bake for 15 minutes.
- To make the dressing, in a blender, combine the garlic clove, raw honey, balsamic vinegar, olive oil and strawberries and blend for 60 seconds.
- Add the results to a jar before adding in the poppy seeds and shaking well.
- Refrigerate for 60 minutes prior to serving.
- Combine all of the chicken salad ingredients together in a large bowl before adding in the dressing and mixing well.
- Add the chicken salad to the paleo rolls prior to serving.

Bibimbap

This recipe needs 8 hours to prepare, requires 90 minutes to cook and will typically make 2 servings.

What to Use-Pork Belly
- Black pepper (as needed)
- Salt (as needed)
- Fish sauce (.25 tsp.)
- Raw honey (2 T)
- Sriracha (.25 cups)
- Coconut vinegar (.5 cups)
- Coconut aminos (.5 cups)
- Pork belly (1 lb. skin removed)

What to Use-Bibimbap
- Sesame seeds (1 T)
- Cilantro (1 handful chopped)
- Green onions (2 sliced)
- Cucumbers (.5 cups sliced)
- Bean sprouts (.5 cups)
- Carrots (.5 cups shredded)
- Kimchi (1 cup)
- Eggs (2)
- Salt (1 pinch)
- Mushrooms (1 cup)
- Coconut oil (2 T)
- Cauliflower rice (2 cups)

What to Do
- To make the pork belly, start by combining all of the ingredients for its sauce together before adding half of that sauce to a sealable plastic bag, adding in the pork belly and shaking well.

Let it chill in the refrigerator for 8 hours.
- Ensure your oven is heated to 450 degrees Fahrenheit.
- Line a baking sheet using tinfoil before topping it with a wire rack. Place the fat side up on the rack and let it bake for 30 minutes. Turn the heat to 225 degrees Fahrenheit and bake for 60 more minutes.
- Let it sit for 5 minutes and cut it into small pieces.
- 30 minutes prior to the pork coming out of the oven, make the cauliflower rice and split it between 2 bowls.
- Add the remainder of the marinade to a pan and place it on the stove above a burner that has been turned to a medium heat. Let it boil and reduce for 10 minutes.
- Add in the pork belly and the sesame seeds and toss well.
- Separately, place a small skillet on top of a burner set to a medium heat before adding in the ghee, a pinch of salt and the mushrooms. Brown the mushrooms and remove them from the pan fore add in the eggs, turning the heat to low and cooking for 6 minutes.
- Assemble the bowls as decided and top with Sriracha prior to serving.

Pork Chile Verde

This recipe needs 45 minutes to prepare, requires 8 hours to cook and will typically make 5 servings.

What to Use
- Black pepper (as needed)
- Salt (as needed)
- Coconut oil (2 T melted)
- Pork bone broth (2 cups)
- White pepper (.5 tsp.)
- Cumin (.5 tsp. ground)
- Red pepper flakes (1 tsp.)
- Oregano (2 tsp.)
- Pork butt (2.5 lbs.)
- Garlic cloves (2 chopped)
- White onion (.25 chopped)
- Lime juice (.5 cups)
- Tomatillos (8 husked, halved)
- Anaheim peppers (3 halved)
- Jalapenos (3 halved)

What to Do
- Ensure that your oven has been preheated to 450 degrees Fahrenheit.
- Add tinfoil to a baking sheet, ensuring it is well covered. Place the halved vegetables on the baking sheet facing downward. Brush the vegetables with coconut oil and top with salt.
- Place the baking sheet in the oven and let it cook for 25 minutes. Let the vegetables cool and peel them.
- In a food processor, add the garlic cloves, onion, lime, peppers and tomatillos before processing well.
- Place a skillet on the stove above a burner that has been turned

to a medium heat. Add in the pork and season as needed before searing it for 5 minutes per side.

- Place the pork butt in the slow cooker before adding in the white pepper, cumin, red pepper flakes, oregano, the results of the food processor and the pork bone broth before covering and letting it cook for 8 hours on a low heat.
- Shred the pork and garnish with cilantro and lime wedges prior to serving.

Braised Pork Chops

This recipe needs 10 minutes to prepare, requires 50 minutes to cook and will typically make 4 servings.

What to Use
- Black pepper (as needed)
- Salt (as needed)
- Coconut oil (2 T)
- Basil (1 T torn)
- Parsley (2 T minced
- Herbs de Provence (1 T)
- Balsamic vinegar (.25 cups)
- Chicken bone broth (.25 cups)
- Tomato sauce (1 cup)
- Tomatoes (28 oz. diced)
- Garlic cloves (3 sliced thin)
- Yellow onion (1 sliced thin)
- Pork chops (4)

What to Do
- Coat a pan with the oil and place it on the stove above a burner that has been turned to a high/medium heat.
- Season the meat as desired before placing the chops in the pan and letting both sides sear for 3 minutes each.
- Remove the pork from the pan before adding in the garlic and onion and letting them cook for 10 minutes, you will know they are finished because the onions will be virtually see through.
- Add in the remaining ingredients besides the basil and cook until the tomatoes begin to break down, about 10 minutes.
- Return the chops to the pan and coat well. Cover the pan and let everything cook for 5 additional minutes.
- Top with sauce prior to serving and serve hot for best results.

Cherry Pork Tenderloin

This recipe needs 5 minutes to prepare, requires 30 minutes to cook and will typically make 3 servings.

What to Use-Pork
- Black pepper (as needed)
- Salt (as needed)
- Coconut oil (2 T)
- Smoked paprika (.25 tsp.)
- Garlic powder (.5 tsp.)
- Pork tenderloin (1.5 lbs.)

What to Use-Cherry Mixture
- Maple syrup (1 T)
- Water (.25 cups)
- Cherries (1 cup pitted)
- Shallot (1 sliced thin)
- Garlic (2 cloves minced)
- Coconut oil (2 T)

What to Do
- Ensure that your oven has been preheated to 400 degrees Fahrenheit.
- Season the tenderloin as desired before coating a skillet in the oil and placing it on the stove above a burner that has been turned to a medium heat. Let the pork cook for 3 minutes on each side.
- Place the skillet in the oven and let it cook until reaches 145 degrees Fahrenheit (12 minutes). Let it sit, covered in foil for 5 minutes.
- Add a sauté pan to the stove over a burner set to a medium heat. Add in the remaining coconut oil before adding the cherries,

shallot and garlic. Toss the results well and let them cook while tossing for 8 minutes.

- Mix in the maple syrup and the water and cook for 3 more minutes.
- Add the cherry mixture to the pork and garnish with parsley prior to serving.

CHAPTER 7

❖

Snack Recipes

Coconut Popsicles

This recipe needs 20 minutes to prepare, requires 12 minutes to cook and will typically make 3 servings.

What to Use
- Cinnamon (.25 tsp.)
- Cardamom (.5 tsp.)
- Vanilla extract (1 tsp.)
- Maple syrup (.25 cups)
- Coconut milk (1 up)
- Pineapple (4 cups diced)
- Caramel sauce (6 tsp.)

What to Do
- Add the pineapple to a blender and blend well. Add the results to a set of popsicle molds so they are filled about a third of the way.
- Add the rest of the blended pineapple to a separate bowl before cleaning out the blender.
- Add the cinnamon, cardamom, vanilla extract, maple syrup and coconut milk to the blender and blend thoroughly. Add the results to the popsicle molds until they are about two-thirds full.

- Add 1 tsp. of caramel to each future popsicle and fill the rest of the mold with the remaining pineapple puree.
- Freeze for 20 minutes prior to serving.

Vanilla Berry Tarts

This recipe needs 30 minutes to prepare, requires 30 minutes to cook and will typically make 5 servings.

What to Use-Crust
- Salt (1 pinch)
- Vanilla extract (1 tsp.)
- Cocoa powder (2 T unsweetened)
- Maple syrup (4 T)
- Ghee (4 T)
- Baking soda (.5 tsp.)
- Tapioca flour (.25 cups + 1 T)
- Coconut flour (.25 cups + 1 T)
- Almond flour (1.5 cups)

What to Use-Vanilla Cream
- Ghee (1 T)
- Vanilla bean (1 beans removed)
- Vanilla extract (1 tsp.)
- Salt (pinch)
- Tapioca flour (.25 cup)
- Maple sugar (.75 cups)
- Egg yolks (5)
- Coconut milk (14 oz.)

What to Use-Glaze
- Lime zest (.5 lime)
- Raw honey (1 T)
- Water (1 T)
- Lime juice (2 limes)

What to Use-Toppings
- Strawberries (.3 cups)
- Raspberries (.3 cups)
- Blackberries (.3 cups)
- Blueberries (.3 cups)

What to Do
- To make the curst, start by preheating your oven to 325 Degrees Fahrenheit.
- Grease 5 tart pans (4 inch)
- Combine all of the crust ingredients in a food processor and process well until it forms a dough.
- Split the dough into fifths and add it to each of the pans, forming it to create a slight bowl shape and poke a few holes in each to prevent it from rising.
- Place the pans in the oven and bake them for 15 minutes. Let them cool for 30 minutes before using.
- To make the vanilla cream, start by adding the coconut milk to a saucepan before placing the pan on the stove on top of a burner set to a medium heat. Let it heat until the milk begins to foam, but not boil.
- At the same time, in a mixing bowl add the maple sugar and egg yolks in a bowl and beat until the results are pale and thick. At this point reduce the seed of the mixer before adding in the salt as well as the tapioca flour and combining well.
- After the milk has foamed, add half of it to the mixing bowl, mixing on a low speed at the same time. Be careful not to scramble the eggs.
- Add the results to the saucepan and whisk until everything thickens which should be approximately 10 minutes.
- Remove from the stove before adding in the vanilla bean, vanilla extract and ghee and mixing thoroughly.

- Add ice to a large bowl until it is full before placing a glass bowl inside of it. Add the cream from the milk to a sieve into the bowl and cover it to cool for 15 minutes.
- For the glaze, combine all of the glaze ingredients and once the cream and crust have finished cooling add in the cream and then the berries.
- Top with the glaze and garnish using powdered sugar and mint leaves prior to serving.

Paleo Cookie Bars

This recipe needs 70 minutes to prepare, requires 18 minutes to cook and will typically make 12 servings.

What to Use-Crust
- Vanilla extract (1 tsp.)
- Maple syrup (4 T)
- Ghee (4 T)
- Baking soda (.5 tsp.)
- Tapioca flour (.25 cups + 1 T)
- Coconut flour (.25 cups + 1 T)
- Almond flour (1.5 cups)

What to Use-Middle Layer
- Salt (1 pinch)
- Vanilla extract (2 tsp.)
- Ghee (2 T)
- Coconut sugar (.75 cups)
- Cashew butter (1.5 cups)

Top layer
- Flaked salt (to taste)
- Chocolate chips (1 cup melted)

What to Do
- Ensure your oven is heated to 325 degrees Fahrenheit.
- Grease a baking dish (8x8).
- Add the crust ingredients to a food processor and process until it turns into dough.
- Place the dough in the pan and place it firmly at the bottom of the pan and putting holes in it to prevent it from rising. Place the pan in the oven and let it cook for 15 minutes.

- Let it cool for 30 minutes prior to use.
- Clean out the food processor before adding in the vanilla extract, ghee, maple sugar and cashew butter and pulse well.
- Add the results to the crust before placing the dish in the freezer for half an hour to harden.
- While it is hardening, melt the chocolate and add it to the top of the dish in a smooth layer.
- Top with salt as desired and let it harden completely before cutting for best results.

Key Lime Parfait

This recipe needs 30 minutes to prepare, requires 12 minutes to cook and will typically make 3 servings.

What to Use-Curd
- Vanilla extract (1 tsp.)
- Ghee (.5 cups)
- Maple sugar (.5 cups)
- Egg yolks (5)
- Key lime juice (.5 cups)
- Key lime zest (.25 cups)

What to Use-Coconut Whipped Cream
- Vanilla extract (1 tsp.)
- Maple syrup (1 T)
- Coconut water (14 oz. chilled)

What to Use-Crust
- Salt (1 pinch)
- Ghee (2 T)
- Maple syrup (1 T)
- Maple sugar (1 T)
- Almond flour (1.5 cups)

What to Do
- To make the key lime curd, in a saucepan, combine the vanilla extract, ghee, maple sugar, egg yolks, lime juice and lime zest. Place the pan on top of a burner set to a low/medium heat and whisk for 10 minutes.
- Add the results to a bowl made of glass before covering the curd tightly with a plastic film. Try and make it air tight. Let it cool to the temperature of the room before setting it in the refrigerator to chill.

- To make the whipped cream, start by removing the cream from the coconut water and adding it to a bowl before adding in the vanilla extract and the maple syrup.
- Add all of the ingredients for the crust to a food processor and process well until it forms a dough.
- Add a base of crust to a small jar, place some of the key lime on top, followed by more curst and then the whipped cream.
- Top with lime zest prior to serving.

Poppy Seed Bread with Strawberries

This recipe needs 20 minutes to prepare, requires 60 minutes to cook and will typically make 1 loaf.

What to Use-Bread
- Poppy seeds (2 T)
- Strawberries (.5 cups sliced)
- Eggs (3 whisked)
- Almond extract (2 tsp.)
- Raw honey (.3 cups)
- Ghee (.3 cups melted)
- Salt (1 pinch)
- Baking powder (.5 tsp.)
- Baking soda (.5 tsp.)
- Arrowroot flour (.25 cups)
- Coconut flour (.25 cups)
- Cashew meal (1.5 cups)
- Zucchini (.5 cups shredded)

What to Use-Sauce
- Water (2 T)
- Raw honey (2 T)
- Lemon juice (2 T)
- Strawberries (1 cup)

What to Do
- Ensure your oven is heated to 350 degrees Fahrenheit.
- Prepare a loaf pan (9x5) by greasing it and lining it with parchment paper.
- Combine the salt, baking powder, baking soda, arrowroot flour, coconut flour and cashew meal in a bowl.
- In a separate bowl combine the eggs, almond extract, raw honey and ghee together and whisk well.

- Mix the two bowls together, add in the strawberries and combine thoroughly.
- Add the results to the loaf pan before placing the pan in the oven and letting it cook for 55 minutes. You will know it is finished when you can stick a toothpick into the loaf and pull it out without encountering any batter.
- Let the bread cool for 10 minutes prior to serving.
- As the bread is baking, add a saucepan to the stove over a burner set to a medium heat. Mix in the sauce ingredients and let them cook for 10 minutes.
- Add the results to a blender and blend until smooth.
- Top the sauce with the bread prior to serving.

Ice Cream Cookie Cups

This recipe needs 20 minutes to prepare, requires 40 minutes to cook and will typically make 14 servings.

What to Use
- Salt (1 pinch)
- Ghee (.25 cups)
- Cinnamon (.25 cinnamon)
- Baking powder (.5 tsp.)
- Vanilla extract (1 tsp.)
- Raw honey (1 T)
- Egg (1)
- Almond flour (1.5 cups)
- Pecans (1 cup)
- Coconut milk ice cream (14 T)
- Chocolate (to taste melted)
- Caramel (to taste melted)

What to Do
- Ensure your oven is heated to 350 degrees Fahrenheit.
- Add the pecans to the food processor and process well before adding in the salt, cinnamon, baking powder, vanilla extract, raw honey, egg, ghee and almond flour.
- Add the results to a mini-muffin tin and ensure that the dough won't rise.
- Place the tin in the oven to cook for 20 minutes and let it cool completely before using.
- Melt the chocolate and caramel for topping the dough with ice cream, chocolate and caramel. Top with sea salt prior to serving.

Caramel Mocha Blended Coffee Drink

This recipe needs 8 hours to prepare, requires 0 minutes to cook and will typically make 2 servings.

What to Use
- Stevia extract (10 drops)
- Vanilla extract (1 tsp.)
- Maple syrup (2 T)
- Almond butter (1 T)
- Cocoa powder (2 T unsweetened)
- Almond milk (.75 cups)
- Caramel (2 T)
- Coffee (1 cup cold brewed)

What to Do
- Freeze the coffee in an ice cube tray.
- In a blender, combine the cubes, stevia, vanilla extract, maple syrup, almond butter, cocoa powder, almond milk and the caramel and blend well.
- Top with coconut whipped cream prior to serving.

Paleo Limeade Mint Cooler

This recipe needs 10 minutes to prepare, requires 0 minutes to cook and will typically make 6 servings.

What to Use
- Stevia (10 drops)
- Ice (4 cups)
- Mint leaves (.3 cups)
- Raw honey (.3 cups)
- Lime juice (.5 cups)
- Lime zest (2 limes)

What to Do
- Add the ice, mint leaves, raw honey, lime juice and lime zest into a blender and blend well.
- Strain the results before adding them to a pitcher and adding in 2 cups of water.
- Mix to combine and garnish with lime wedges prior to serving.

Thai Iced Tea

This recipe needs 10 minutes to prepare, requires 20 minutes to cook and will typically make 4 servings.

What to Use-Tea
- Vanilla extract (.5 tsp.)
- Stevia extract (20 drops)
- Maple syrup (.3 cups)
- Cloves (2)
- Cinnamon (1 stick)
- Anise stars (3)
- Black tea bags (4)
- Water (4 cups)

What to Use-Coconut Milk
- Vanilla bean (.5 halved, deseeded)
- Vanilla extract (.5 tsp.)
- Maple syrup (2 T)
- Coconut milk (2 cups)

What to Do
- Add the water to a saucepan before placing in on the stove over a burner set to a high heat. Let the water boil before adding in the tea ingredients and letting it steep for approximately 20 minutes.
- Strain the tea and let it cool for a minimum of 20 minutes. After it has cooled, add in the vanilla means, vanilla extract and coconut milk and whisk well.
- Add ice to each serving glass, mix together a .75/.25 mixture of tea and coconut milk.

Paleo Banana Smoothie

This recipe needs 5 minutes to prepare, requires 0 minutes to cook and will typically make 2 servings.

What to Use
- Chia seeds (.5 T)
- Vanilla extract (.5 tsp.)
- Coconut extract (.5 tsp.)
- Vanilla protein powder (2 T)
- Almond milk (1.5 cups)
- Coconut cream (.6 cups)
- Pineapple (1 cup cubed, frozen)
- Banana (1 frozen)

What to Do
- Add all of the ingredients for the smoothie into a blender before blending until the contents are smooth.
- Split into 2 glasses, serve and enjoy.

Paleo Pumpkin Smoothie

This recipe needs 5 minutes to prepare, requires 0 minutes to cook and will typically make 2 servings.

What to Use
- Chia seeds (.5 T)
- Vanilla extract (.5 tsp.)
- Coconut extract (.5 tsp.)
- Vanilla protein powder (2 T)
- Almond milk (1.5 cups)
- Pumpkin pie spice (5 tsp.)
- Maple syrup (1 T)
- Pumpkin puree (.3 cups)
- Banana (1 frozen)

What to Do
- Add all of the ingredients for the smoothie into a blender before blending until the contents are smooth.
- Split into 2 glasses, serve and enjoy.

Paleo Chocolate Smoothie

This recipe needs 5 minutes to prepare, requires 0 minutes to cook and will typically make 2 servings.

What to Use
- Chia seeds (.5 T)
- Vanilla extract (.5 tsp.)
- Coconut extract (.5 tsp.)
- chocolate protein powder (2 T0
- Almond milk (1.5 cups)
- Raw honey (1 T)
- Cocoa powder (1 tsp.)
- Cherries (1 cup frozen, pitted)
- Banana (1 frozen)

What to Do
- Add all of the ingredients for the smoothie into a blender before blending until the contents are smooth.
- Split into 2 glasses, serve and enjoy.

Paleo Strawberry Smoothie

This recipe needs 5 minutes to prepare, requires 0 minutes to cook and will typically make 2 servings.

What to Use
- Chia seeds (.5 T)
- Vanilla extract (.5 tsp.)
- Coconut extract (.5 tsp.)
- Vanilla protein powder (2 T0
- Almond milk (.6 cups)
- Strawberries (.5 cups frozen)
- Orange juice (.5 cups)
- Banana (1 frozen)

What to Do
- Add all of the ingredients for the smoothie into a blender before blending until the contents are smooth.
- Split into 2 glasses, serve and enjoy.

Sweet Potato Coffee

This recipe needs 5 minutes to prepare, requires 0 minutes to cook and will typically make 2 servings.

What to Use
- Chia seeds (1 T)
- Coffee (1 tsp. ground)
- Vanilla extract (1 tsp.)
- Raw honey (1 T)
- Vanilla protein powder (1 scoop)
- Almond milk (2 cups)
- Sweet potato (1 cup frozen)

What to Do
- Add all of the ingredients into a blender before blending until the contents are smooth.
- Split into 2 glasses, serve and enjoy.

Conclusion

❖

Thank you again for reading this book! I hope this book was able to help you to learn everything you could want to know about the paleo diet and how following it can help you both look and feel better than you ever thought possible. Remember, once you get started on the recipes above it is important to give your body the time it needs to really adjust to your new lifestyle before making any decisions as to its long term efficacy when it comes to your own body. Given time, odds are you won't want to go back.

The next step is to stop reading and start cooking. The recipes in the proceeding chapters should be considered building blocks on which you can expand. Keep trying new options and you never know when you are going to find a new favorite.

Finally, if you enjoyed this book, then I'd like to ask you for a favor, would you be kind enough to leave a review for this book on Amazon? It'd be greatly appreciated!

Made in the USA
San Bernardino, CA
25 May 2017